CPSIA information can be obtained
at www.ICGtesting.com
Printed in the USA
BVHW052256170722
642384BV00005B/358 9 781669 512264